THE COOLEST CHINESE
Architecture

Therese M. Shea

CRAZY
COOL
CHINA

ROSEN
PUBLISHING

SinolinguA
华语教学出版社

NEW YORK   BEIJING

Published in 2022 by The Rosen Publishing Group, Inc.
29 East 21st Street, New York, NY 10010

Jointly published in 2022 by Sinolingua Co.,Ltd., Beijing, China, and The Rosen Publishing Group, Inc., New York, New York, United States.

First Edition

Editor: Therese Shea
Designer: Rachel Rising

Photo credits: cover, testing/Shutterstock.com; cover, pp. 1–48 Sylfida/Shutterstock.com; cover, p. 1 CkyBe/Shutterstock.com; pp. 4, 6, 10, 14, 18, 22, 26, 30, 34, 38, 42 Ben Bryant/Shutterstock.com; p. 5 QinJin/Shutterstock.com; p. 7 LP2 Studio/Shutterstock.com; p. 8 Huang Zheng/Shutterstock.com; p. 11 Songquan Deng/Shutterstock.com; p. 12 TonyV3112/Shutterstock.com; p. 12 Adam Yee/Shutterstock.com; pp. 15, 16, 28, 43 Imaginechina/Imaginechina Limited/Alamy Stock Photo; p. 16 Kirill Neiezhmakov/Shutterstock.com; pp. 19, 20 Jianan Yu/Reuters/Newscom; p. 23 GuoZhongHua/Shutterstock.com; p. 24 Sun Xuejun/Shutterstock.com; p. 27 Legacy Entertainment; p. 31 https://commons.wikimedia.org/wiki/File:Chongqing_Art_Museum_20150313.jpg; p. 32 LP2 Studio/Shutterstock.com; p. 35 Eric Lafforgue/Alamy Stock Photo; p. 36 Frumm John/hemis.fr/Hemis/Alamy Stock Photo; pp. 39, 40 4045/Shutterstock.com.

Some of the images in this book illustrate individuals who are models. The depictions do not imply actual situations or events.

Cataloging-in-Publication Data
Names: Shea, Therese M.
Title: The coolest Chinese architecture / Therese M. Shea.
Description: New York : Rosen Young Adult, 2022. | Series: Crazy cool China | Includes glossary and index.
Identifiers: ISBN 9781499472394 (pbk.) | ISBN 9781499472400 (library bound) | ISBN 9781499472417 (ebook)
Subjects: LCSH: Architecture–China–Juvenile literature.
Classification: LCC NA1540.S43 2022 | DDC 720.951–dc23

Manufactured in the United States of America

CPSIA Compliance Information: Batch #CSRYA23. For further information, contact Rosen Publishing, New York, New York, at 1-800-237-9932.

Find us on

Contents

Centuries
of Incredible Architecture

The attributes of ancient Chinese architecture are recognizable around the world. Towering tiered **pagodas**. Temples with roofs curving up to the corners. Deliberate use of colors, such as yellow for royalty and red for good fortune. These are just some of the visually striking architectural details that are plainly and uniquely Chinese. Hundreds of years of traditional construction brought change, but builders still adhered to some basic features, including symmetrical arrangements;

Feng shui, which translates as "wind water" in Chinese, is an ancient practice of arranging buildings, objects, and space to achieve balance and harmony. The Chinese have been designing their homes, towns, and burial places using feng shui principles for over 4,000 years. Simple examples include having a view of water or a south-facing door. A prominent modern structure that utilizes feng shui principles is the HSBC Building of Hong Kong.

wooden materials; wide, low buildings; a balance between natural and man-made surroundings; and an accordance with feng shui guidelines.

While modern Chinese architects still consider and implement some of these characteristics in their designs, particularly in rural areas, the nation's rapid urban development in the twentieth and twenty-first centuries has demanded innovative ideas. Internationally known architects have been invited to participate in the country's landmark construction projects as well. The result is some of the most admired, surprising, and jaw-dropping structures in the world.

Because so many ancient Chinese buildings were made of wood, like this pagoda, few have survived. However, models have been found in tombs.

New Century Global Center

Sometimes when searching for amazing buildings, architecture fans look for the tallest. But there's another measure of size that is equally as impressive: floor area. To see the largest building in that category, you would need to travel to Chengdu in China's Sichuan province. That's the home of the New Century Global Center. Completed in 2013, it's the largest man-made structure in the world by floor area. The building is 1,640 feet (500 meters) long, 1,312 feet (400 m) wide, and 328 feet (100 m) high—and is 420 acres (170 hectares) in all!

How large is the New Century Global Center? It's 18.4 million square feet (1.7 million square meters). And how large is that? Have you ever seen the Pentagon in Virginia, near Washington, DC? Three Pentagons could fit inside the Sichuan structure. What about the Sydney Opera House? Twenty of those could fit inside!

The center is made of glass and steel, which reflect its surroundings. While that alone is attention grabbing, the structure's unusual wavy roof will catch the eye of any passing pedestrian.

It might be hard to tell how big the New Century Global Center actually is when looking at a photograph. It's four times larger than the smallest country in the world: Vatican City.

The New Century Global Center is situated above a subway station for easy access.

A New Century Global Center guide named Liu Xun gave an interview to the *Sydney Morning Herald* when the structure opened. He explained one of the center's most unusual features: "There will be an artificial sun that will shine 24 hours a day and allow for a comfortable temperature. The system uses specialized lighting technology that heats as well as illuminates."

The New Century Global Center is a multipurpose building. In fact, visitors can find more than a few things to do inside. As they enter at the front, they step into a lobby 213 feet (65 m) high. They then can choose to shop in one of China's largest malls, see a movie at a 14-screen **IMAX** theater, skate on an Olympic-sized ice rink, or stay overnight in one of 2,000 rooms at the two luxury hotels within.

If that's not exciting enough, visitors can check out Paradise Island Waterpark. This indoor attraction has a sand beach over 1,300 feet (396 m) long. The world's largest **LED** screen projects images of the horizon to help transport beachgoers' imaginations.

Not everything about the New Century Global Center is about leisure and pleasure, though. A business tower within the building offers over 7 million square feet (650,000 sq m) of office space.

Beijing National Stadium

When a country hosts the Olympic Games, it hopes to shine a spotlight on its culture and its accomplishments. It wants to both inspire and be admired by the millions who are watching the elite athletes. Often that means building world-class athletic facilities for Olympic events. Perhaps the most memorable Olympic structure of the last century is Beijing National Stadium, constructed for the 2008 Summer Games. Sometimes it's better known as the "Bird's Nest," as that's what it closely resembles. However, the

> When searching for inspiration for the national stadium, the designers studied a Chinese pottery technique called crazing. It produces a network of fine cracks in the glaze on ceramics. However, while the pattern of steel parts looks random, it's carefully planned. Some pieces are simply functional, while others are necessary for structural **integrity**.

National Stadium's **elliptical** shape is meant to represent heaven. (The nearby National Aquatics Center is square, a reflection of the Chinese symbol for Earth.)

The stadium consists of two main structures. Within is a concrete bowl supported by 24 main columns, each weighing 1,000 tons (907 metric tons). Around it, at a distance of about 50 feet (15 m), is a frame made of twisting sections of steel, which are the "twigs" of the nest-like stadium. Both are fixed to a joint foundation.

The stadium was designed by architects Jacques Herzog and Pierre de Meuron, project architect Stefan Marbach, artist Ai Weiwei, and chief architect Li Xinggang of China Architecture Design and Research Group (CADG).

The National Stadium will host the Olympics again—this time the Winter Games—in 2022. Preparations for Winter Olympic events are shown below.

Beijing is in one of the world's most active **seismic** zones, so it was important for the stadium to be unaffected by major shocks. The design was created with earthquakes in mind and the stadium itself tested. The roof was separated from the seating bowl to further ensure that the structure was earthquake resistant.

Beijing National Stadium extends about 965 feet (294 m) from east to west and 1,093 feet (333 m) from north to south, and has a height of 226 feet (69 m). The steel frame remains the largest all-steel structure in the world. It weighs about 42,000 tons (38,100 mt) and covers 2,740,492 square feet (254,600 sq m). The stadium contains 91,000 permanent seats with space for another 11,000.

The opening and closing ceremonies and athletic track and field events of the Summer Olympics took place at the stadium. It's also used as a soccer (or football) field and has underground pipes installed beneath for a **geothermal** heating system. In winter, the system absorbs the heat from the soil, which aids in heating the stadium. In summer, the system uses the chilly temperatures of the soil to cool the stadium.

Fang Yuan Building

Architects get inspiration from many spheres of life—nature, history, and other structures, to name a few. Famous architect C. Y. Lee was inspired for the design of a building in Shenyang, the capital of Liaoning province in the northeast, by an ancient Chinese coin. The building's name, Fang Yuan, means "square" and "round," which reflects the shapes of the Chinese coin, a circle with a square cut from its middle. And, indeed, the building has both shapes represented. In fact, from the side, it looks like a row of copper coins atop a rectangular block.

C. Y. Lee is an architect of many accomplishments. Perhaps the most famous is the skyscraper Taipei 101 in Chinese Taipei. It was the tallest building in the world from 2004 to 2010 and is still the tallest in Chinese Taipei, reaching a height of 1,667 feet (508 m).

Completed in 2001, the Fang Yuan Building, sometimes called the Fang Yuan Mansion, is a 24-floor office building, with 22 floors above the ground and 2 floors underground. Its total height is 327 feet (100 m).

The Fang Yuan Building contains about 516,668 square feet (48,000 sq m) of floor space.

The square on the front of the Fang Yuan Building isn't visible from the back.

Aldar Headquarters in Abu Dhabi

The Fang Yuan Building is actually not the only building in the world with this two-dimensional coin shape. The Aldar Headquarters in Abu Dhabi, United Arab Emirates, has a similar form. Its architect, Marwan Zgheib, was inspired by the shape of a clamshell. The result is a gleaming round skyscraper with a curved glass skin.

The Fang Yuan Building is a cause of great debate. It's been ranked as one of the world's "ugliest buildings" by news organizations such as CNN and *Time*. Some think the suggestion of money in the building's design is distasteful. And still others think the structure's round shape is just too odd in the midst of Shenyang's traditional buildings. However, many appreciate the thoughtfulness behind the design and its unique **silhouette**. In fact, the controversial design has given the structure some **notoriety**. The businesses that occupy the Fang Yuan Building appreciate the publicity.

A Shenyang inhabitant named Wang Huan summed up the building's impact well in the *China Daily* newspaper: "It has a wow factor. It's **susceptible** to **aesthetic** criticism but never fails to shock."

The Piano House

If a coin-shaped building seems strange, a house shaped like a grand piano might seem even stranger. Perhaps even stranger than that is its entrance—a giant upright violin leaning against the piano shape.

This "Piano House" is located in Huainan, which is in China's Anhui province. Built in 2007, it was designed by the architecture students of Hefei University of Technology to encourage tourism in the city. The outside of the building is mostly clad in transparent and black glass panels. White and black glass panes on one side of the building look like the keys of a piano.

The Piano House was built to attract attention—and tourists—and it has. People often visit to have their photo taken in front of the building. In fact, it's become a popular place for newlyweds to have their picture taken. This is so true that it's sometimes called "the most romantic building in China."

The "piano" is raised off the ground by three concrete pillars, giving the impression of piano legs beneath a grand piano. People lounge underneath in the shade of the building during the day. The rooftop terrace, too, gives shade with a special feature: it looks like the open lid of the piano.

The Piano House is built at a scale of 50:1, which means that the "instruments" of the building are exactly 50 times larger than a real grand piano and violin.

Neon lights line the outside edges of the building, to stunning effect at night.

As distinctive as the Piano House is, it's not the only structure inspired by the shape of a musical instrument. The Grand Guitar (demolished) was a three-story guitar-shaped museum, as well as a music and gift shop, in Bristol, Tennessee. It was the only such building in the United States until the Guitar Hotel in Hollywood, Florida, was completed in 2019. It's 450 feet (137 m) tall and contains 638 rooms and suites!

The violin section of the Piano House is completely see-through, with clear windows allowing visitors to observe people ascending and descending the escalators and stairs leading into and out of the main building.

The Piano House isn't actually a house. Unsurprisingly, it has some musical purposes. The bottom part of the "piano" contains two concert halls. Rooms within are also used as a practice space for musicians at local colleges. In addition, the Piano House holds an office and **exhibition** space for Huainan city planners to display their work and future development plans.

And it's not just the outside of the Piano House that's spectacular. From within the building, people have an impressive view of the city of Huainan.

National Center for the Performing Arts

The arts have always been an important part of China, ancient and modern. To show the country's commitment to the performing arts, the largest theater complex in all of Asia was built in Beijing between 2001 and 2006. Called the National Center for the Performing Arts (NCPA), it's not only impressive for its size but also its curved steel exterior—a whopping 1,609,205 square feet (149,500 sq m). Surrounded by a man-made lake, it seems like it's an emerging island to onlookers.

Sometimes called "the Egg," the NCPA is a dome measuring 696 feet (212 m) east to west and 472 feet (144 m) north to south. The exterior is made of about 18,000 titanium plates—and only four plates are the same shape. The middle part of the shell is transparent and uses 1,000 sheets of special glass.

Inside the structure are an opera house, concert hall, theater, art exhibition halls, restaurants, and other facilities. These spaces aren't small, either. Of the performance auditoriums, the opera house seats 2,091 people, the concert hall 1,859 people, and the theater 957. From the outside, the NCPA doesn't seem large enough. That's because this building, ingeniously designed by French architect Paul Andreu, has a large section that's completely underground.

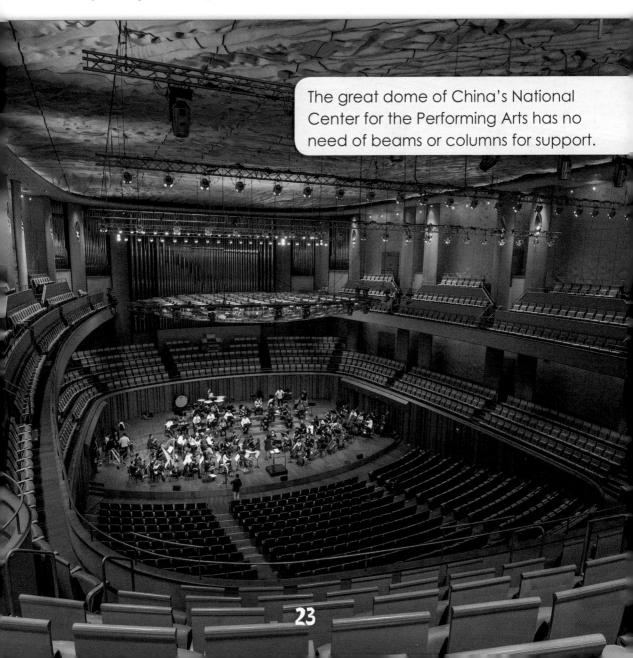

The great dome of China's National Center for the Performing Arts has no need of beams or columns for support.

The reflection of the glowing building at night is a breathtaking sight.

The National Center for the Performing Arts is located to the west of the Great Hall of the People and near the Forbidden City. At first, some thought it was too modern for this section of the city. But architect Paul Andreu insisted the area should include modern architecture too. However, he intentionally included traditional touches, such as trees and large open spaces too. The foyer is covered in stone from 10 different regions of China, in a nod to national pride.

The NCPA is partially underground for a reason. No building in the vicinity can be taller than the Great Hall of the People, which is used for important government functions. Out of respect for that regulation, the NCPA is about 10 stories deep and about 152 feet (46.3 m) high above the ground, just a bit shorter than the Great Hall.

All entrances to the main building are through the water. If people travel by way of the north entrance, they'll descend the grand staircase, which stretches 260 feet (80 m), while above them, the light from the outside shimmers through the lake water. And surrounding the lake is around 419,790 square feet (39,000 sq m) of green space, a "green belt" allowing visitors to experience a tranquil walk before or after seeing a performance.

The Ring of Life

All the structures you've read about so far have been places for people to occupy. The next example is a bit different. The Ring of Life is a steel monument in Shenfu New Town, in northeast China's Liaoning province. The community of Shenfu New Town is indeed a "new town." Its plans were laid out in 2009 between the two rapidly growing industrial cities of Shenyang and Fushun. It was hoped that Shenfu New Town could be a place for the ever-expanding populations of the cities to inhabit.

Designer Gary Goddard explained the ring's meaning to the region: "The Ring of Life rises as a unique emblem of the goals and aspirations of this new city's founders. The ring is a metaphor for the balance in all things, and despite the classic simplicity of a perfect circle, none of the world's iconic structures and monuments had embodied it until now. I felt this classic symbol, set at the edge of the lake and the urban street, best represented the spirit of Shenfu New City."

One of the agencies brought in to design a part of Shenfu New Town was a California firm called the Goddard Group, led by Gary Goddard. It was Goddard himself who came up with the idea of constructing an immense steel ring, and local authorities liked the notion, hoping it would attract tourists to their new city.

Besides the Ring of Life, shown here, the Goddard Group has helped design theme parks, resorts, and **casinos**.

The original design of the Ring of Life included a bungee-jumping platform at its top. However, it was judged to be too high for such an activity.

The Ring of Life succeeded in one purpose at least—it drew a lot of notice. However, it didn't just attract tourists to Shenfu New Town. It also attracted internet attention. Some people thought it was odd, and others admired it. Still others manipulated funny pictures of the steel ring, making it look like cats or spaceships were going through it!

Goddard explained that the local planners had asked his group to create a "heart" for the center of Shenfu New Town. The Ring of Life was built at a place where a river, two lakes, and the city's midpoint converged. It was meant to be a permanent reminder of how nature and man-made structures can exist in harmony and balance.

The ring was completed in 2012. It stands about 515 feet (157 m) tall and weighs about 3,000 tons (2,722 mt). Around 12,000 LED lights dot its surface, lighting up the ring at night in different colors. Four elevators within the ring can transport visitors to an observation deck at the top.

The Chongqing Art Museum

The Chongqing Art Museum mainly houses traditional art forms, including paintings, prints, and sculptures. However, the museum looks far from traditional, at least at first glance. Located in the city of Chongqing in southwestern China, the building appears to have been made by weaving together red and black rods. The black rods run east to west, and the red rods run north to south.

The building's architects say that the inspiration from the design partly comes from traditional Chinese structures with layered interlocking wooden

The Chongqing Art Museum is located in the Liberation Monument area of Chongqing, the city's commercial and financial center. The monument was built in 1945 to memorialize the victory of China over Japan in the Second Sino-Japanese War. It was renamed Chongqing People's Liberation Monument to commemorate the occupation of the city of Chongqing by the People's Liberation Army.

brackets, though perhaps not in such a bold way. The rods aren't purely decorative, however. About 40 percent are used to serve as vents in the building's air-conditioning system.

The Chongqing Art Museum is sometimes known as the Chongqing Art Gallery or the Chongqing Guotai Arts Center.

The Chongqing Art Museum opened in 2013.

The interior of the museum is exquisite as well. Glass-encased rooms accommodate smaller exhibits, while the exhibition hall on the fifth floor is more than 20,000 square feet (1,850 sq m). A red winding steel staircase in the middle of the exhibition hall connects visitors with the sixth floor and gives them a feeling of climbing to the uppermost heights of the city.

The Chongqing Art Museum took eight years to build, a long time compared to similar construction projects in the nation. The structure was carefully designed to fit into the crowded Yuzhong District of the city by the architecture firm China Architecture Design & Research Group. This included its colors. Red symbolizes the warmhearted Chongqing people, while black represents the history of the ancient Bayu culture of the area. The structure covers over 882,640 square feet (82,000 sq m).

From a certain distance, the building is said to look like a fig tree, a plant common in the region, once again connecting China's urban architecture to nature. Other people say that the red beams make the building look like it's on fire. In any case, it attracts the eye among the many modern buildings of Chongqing.

The Commune by the Great Wall

An architectural wonder *by* an architectural wonder. That's how one could most appropriately explain the Commune by the Great Wall. It's a **boutique** hotel near the Great Wall of China that's made up of many villas with over 100 suites and 11 presidential suites. Each villa has a different structure and theme.

For example, the Forest House looks like a bird's nest in a tree, while the Airport House has three living rooms that extend in different directions—just like the corridors of an airport. The Cantilever House (called the "Red House" in Chinese) features a wooden walkway that winds

You might wonder what a villa and a suite are. A villa is another name for a residence with well-maintained grounds. Villas have traditionally been a retreat from city life. A suite is a group of rooms, and a presidential suite is a suite considered fit for a president or other high-ranking person.

around an inner courtyard, over a grassy slope, to a rooftop terrace with gorgeous views of the mountains.

And the Bamboo Wall House was built with the stiff-stemmed, woody plant as the primary material. The designer, Japanese architect Kengo Kuma, liked the **juxtaposition** of the Great Wall's hard, heavy stone and the building's light, delicate bamboo.

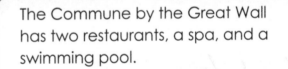

The Commune by the Great Wall has two restaurants, a spa, and a swimming pool.

Great Wall of China

The villas of the Commune by the Great Wall are located in a green valley near the Great Wall. Residents can hike to an ancient section of the wall.

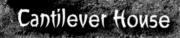

Cantilever House

The Great Wall of China is one of the biggest structures ever made by humans. Built to stop the enemy armies, the first parts were constructed in the 600s BCE. The wall that still stands today winds across China for about 5,500 miles (8,850 km). At any given section, its height is from 15 to 30 feet (4.5 to 9 m), and its width is 15 to 25 feet (4.5 to 7.5 m).

How did each villa get such a unique look? The entire project was the idea of Zhang Xin, a Chinese real estate developer. She sought out 12 architects from different parts of Asia and requested that they each design a home for people seeking refuge from the busy urban life of Beijing, which is a little over an hour's drive away. What resulted were a dozen beautifully designed villas. The project won a special architecture award at the Venice Biennale, a prestigious arts organization in Italy, in 2002.

Today, there are 40 villas; most are **replicas** of the original structures. To attract families with children, a "kid's club" was added in 2007, which includes a library, **recreational** area, TV rooms, and more.

Thames Town

Imagine traveling southwest out of the bustling downtown area of Shanghai. You'll pass countless gleaming modern buildings. About 20 miles (32 km) outside the city's central area, the architecture becomes quite different. In fact, you might think you've left the country—or even the continent. If you find yourself on **cobblestone** streets surrounded by British homes and shops, you're probably in Thames Town.

The original plan—called the One City, Nine Towns initiative—called for nine districts in all to be built around Shanghai's suburbs. Other designs imitated the Western architecture of Italy, Spain, Holland, Norway, and Germany. The communities born from this initiative aren't the only tributes to Western designs in China. There's even an "Eiffel Tower"!

In 2001, a planning commission in Shanghai sought a plan to lure some of its residents outside the jam-packed city. A proposal was submitted: make suburbs that look like cities of Western regions. The Shanghai group hosted a global design competition to award the contracts. For Thames Town, the British firm Atkins won the bid for design, while Shanghai Songjiang New City Construction was enlisted to build the design.

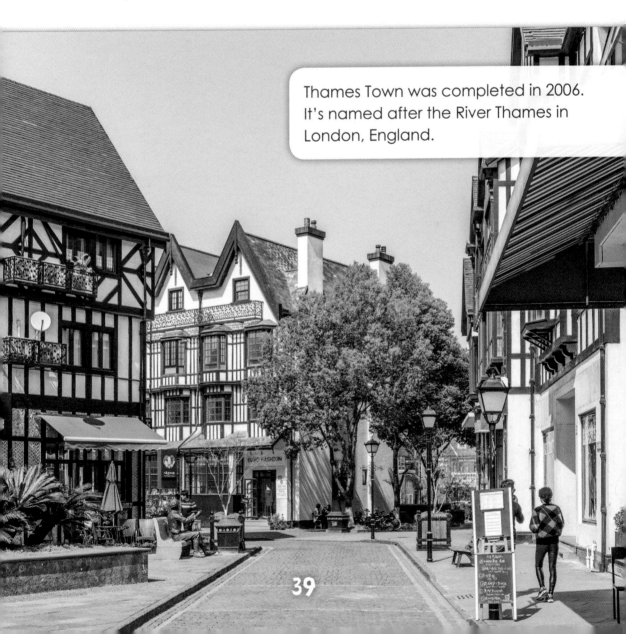

Thames Town was completed in 2006. It's named after the River Thames in London, England.

About 500 years of British architecture can be seen within the confines of Thames Town.

As the Shanghai Planning Commission hoped, people were extremely interested in owning a home in Thames Town. Units sold quickly. However, the housing costs proved to be too high for the middle-income residents that the commission had wanted to appeal to. Instead, wealthy people bought homes as investment properties or as second homes rather than their primary property. Thames Town hasn't become a flourishing suburb quite yet.

less than 1/2 square mile (1.3 sq km). However, a lot is packed into the small space! A replica of the historic Christ Church of Bristol, England, was **meticulously** erected, as well as Edwardian-style townhomes and a Tudor-style pub. Gothic and Victorian structures are a mere walk away from each other. Lampposts were imported from Great Britain, and red phone booths, a James Bond statue, and many more landmarks can be spotted within the community.

But Thames Town isn't just about sights. The architects included all the other things a town needs to survive and thrive, including schools, stores, and recreational areas.

The T30 Hotel

The T30 Hotel in the city of Changsha, Hunan, is striking, but more remarkable is the time it took to build—just 15 days! The typical time to erect such a building is over a year.

The project was undertaken by Broad Sustainable Building, a corporation specializing in environmentally friendly and earthquake-resistant structures. The materials used were 90 percent prefabricated, manufactured off-site, saving a lot of time. It took just 46 hours for the builders to finish the main structure.

The building of the T30 Hotel became a viral internet sensation when Broad Sustainable released a time-lapse video of the construction. In a matter of minutes, people can watch the sped-up construction of the 328-foot (100 m) tower on China's Hunan River, which, in real time, occurred over just 360 hours. Broad Sustainable's founder and president, Zhang Yue, stated in an interview with *Wired* magazine, "It's a structural revolution."

Why prefabricated? Less waste. According to Broad Sustainable, a traditional high-rise produces about 3,000 tons (2,722 mt) of construction waste, while a Broad Sustainable building produces 25 tons (23 mt). The Broad Sustainable method is less expensive too.

One of Broad Sustainable's next projects is to assemble Sky City One, a 220-floor building in Changsha—in 90 days. If successful, it would be the world's tallest building. Clearly, Chinese architecture will continue to impress with its concepts and creations.

The China Academy of Building Research asserts the T30 Hotel is five times more earthquake-resistant than standard buildings. The T30 also uses less concrete and less structural steel to reduce weight.

aesthetic Relating to art or beauty.

boutique Offering services of a high quality to a small number of customers.

casino A club, or a room in a club, hotel, or other place, where gambling takes place.

cobblestone A naturally rounded stone larger than a pebble and smaller than a boulder.

elliptical Shaped like an oval.

exhibition A public showing of works of art.

geothermal Relating to or using the heat of Earth's interior.

IMAX A system of high-resolution cameras, film formats, film projectors, and theaters known for having very large, tall screens.

integrity The state of being complete or whole.

juxtaposition The act of placing two or more things side by side to compare or contrast them or to create an interesting effect.

LED A semiconductor diode that produces light when a voltage is applied to it, used especially in electronic devices.

meticulously In a manner marked by extreme care in the treatment of details.

notoriety The condition of being well known for an undesirable reason.

pagoda A structure common in eastern Asia resembling a richly decorated tower, typically with curved roofs, that was usually erected as a temple or memorial.

recreational Relating to relaxation or fun.

replica A reproduction or copy of something.

seismic Relating to or caused by an earthquake.

silhouette A representation of the outline of an object.

susceptible Likely to be influenced or affected.

For More Information

American Institute of Architects (AIA)
1735 New York Ave NW
Washington, DC 20006-5292
(800) AIA-3837
Website: www.aia.org/
The AIA strives to spread information about how architects have a responsibility to design a better future for the U.S. and the planet.

Beijing Ancient Architecture Museum
21 Dongjing Road
Xuanwu District
Beijing, P. R. China
This is the first museum in China to display ancient Chinese architectural technology, art, and history.

Broad Sustainable Building
BROAD Town
Hunan District
Changsha, P. R. China 410138
Websites: en.broad.com/
www.broad.com/
Learn more about the Chinese company that's revolutionizing the process of construction.

MAD Architects
8F, Tower A, No. 107 North Dongsi Street
Dongcheng District
Beijing, P. R. China

2056 Broadway
Santa Monica, CA 90404
(310) 776-9680
Website: www.i-mad.com/

This global architecture firm focuses on the development of technologically advanced designs that embody humankind's attraction to nature.

National Building Museum
401 F Street NW
Washington, DC 20001
info@nbm.org
(202) 272-2448
Website: www.nbm.org/
The National Building Museum invites visitors to experience the world that people both design and build through exhibitions and more.

National Center for the Performing Arts (NCPA)
No. 2 West Chang'an Avenue
Xicheng District
Beijing, P. R. China
Website: en.chncpa.org/
The NCPA is the celebrated home of performing arts in Beijing and China as a whole. Check out its website to see more of its stunning design—and to find out what's playing.

Washington Architectural Foundation
421 7th Street NW
Washington, DC 20004
(202) 347-9403
Website: www.aiadc.com/waf
The Washington Architectural Foundation serves many groups: students, teachers, professionals, and the public. Check out its online learning resources.

Andong Lu and Pingping Dou. *China Homegrown: Chinese Experimental Architecture Reborn*. Oxford, UK: John Wiley & Sons, 2018.

Calder, Barnabas. *Architecture: From Prehistory to Climate Emergency*. London, UK: Pelican, 2021.

Herron, Pamela. *Exploring Ancient China*. Mankato, MN: 12-Story Library, 2018.

Jones, Grace. *The Greatest Buildings and Structures*. New York, NY: Crabtree Publishing Company, 2019.

Kenney, Karen Latchana. *Mysteries of the Great Wall of China*. Minneapolis, MN: Lerner Publications, 2018.

Klanten, Robert, Elli Stuhler, and Shu Wang. *Beauty and the East*. Berlin, Germany: Gestalten, 2021.

Klanten, Robert, et al. *Beyond the West: New Global Architecture*. Berlin, Germany: Gestalten, 2020.

Knapp, Ronald G., et al. *China's Covered Bridges: Architecture over Water*. Shanghai, China: Jiaoda Art Publishing, 2019.

Li Xiangning and Jiang Jiawei. *Architecture China: Building for a New Culture*. New York, NY: Images Publishing Group Pty, 2019.

Provoost, Kris. *Beautified China: The Architectural Revolution*. Tielt, Belgium: Lannoo Publishers, 2019.

Steiner, Henriette, and Kristin Veel. *Tower to Tower: Gigantism in Architecture and Digital Culture*. Cambridge, MA: MIT Press, 2020.

Steinhardt, Nancy Shatzman. *Chinese Architecture: A History*. Princeton, NJ: Princeton University Press, 2019.

Tong, Jialin. *Eco China: Roof Gardens and Green Walls*. London, UK: Design Media Publishing, 2019.

Van Uffelen, Chris. *Young Visionaries: The New Generation of Architects*. Salenstein, Switzerland: Braun Publishing AG, 2019.

Wang Jian and Fang Xiaoyan. *An Illustrated Brief History of China: Culture, Religion, Art, Invention*. La Vergne, TN: Tuttle Publishing, 2020.

Williams, Austin. *China's Urban Revolution: Understanding Chinese Eco-Cities*. London, UK: Bloomsbury Publishing, 2020.

Williams, Austin, and Zhang Xin. *New Chinese Architecture: Twenty Women Building the Future*. London, UK: Thames & Hudson, 2019.

Yanxin Cai. *Chinese Architecture*. Beijing, China: China Intercontinental Press, 2018.

Bibliography

Adams, William Lee. "15 Buildings That Don't Look Like Buildings." *Time*. November 5, 2012. https://www.chinadaily.com.cn/week-end/2014-11/08/content_18886853.htm.

Andrews, Kate. "World's Largest Building Opens in China." *Dezeen*. July 13, 2019. https://www.dezeen.com/2013/07/10/worlds-largest-building-opens-chengdu-china/.

ArchDaily.com. "National Grand Theater of China/Paul Andreu." Undated. Retrieved August 12, 2021. https://www.archdaily.com/1218/national-grand-theater-of-china-paul-andreu.

Arup.com. "Chinese National Stadium (Bird's Nest)." Undated. Retrieved July 22, 2021. https://www.arup.com/projects/chinese-nation-al-stadium.

Goddard Group. "Designer Gary Goddard's 'Ring of Life' Attracts Global Attention as Emblem of China's Master-Planned City of Shenfu New Town." PR Newswire. December 12, 2012. https://www.prnewswire.com/news-releases/designer-gary-goddards-ring-of-life-attracts-global-attention-as-emblem-of-chinas-master-planned-city-of-shenfu-new-town-184101551.html.

Hilgers, Lauren. "Meet the Man Who Built a 30-Story Building in 15 Days." *Wired*. September 25, 2012. https://www.wired.com/2012/09/broad-sustain-able-building-instant-skyscraper/.

Jackson, Joe. "Chinese Builders Construct 30-Story Hotel—In 15 Days." *Time*. January 20, 2012. https://newsfeed.time.com/2012/01/10/chinese-builders-construct-30-story-hotel-in-15-days/. builders-construct-30-story-hotel-in-15-days/.

Jennings, Ken. "The British Ghost Town in the Middle of China." *Condé Nast Traveler*. January 4, 2016. https://www.cntraveler.com/stories/2016-01-04/the-english-ghost-town-in-the-middle-of-china.

Liang Ssu-ch'eng. *Chinese Architecture: A Pictorial History*, edited by Wilma Fairbank. Mineola, NY: Dover Publications, 2005.

Nilsson, Erik, et al. "Beautiful ... or Ugly? In China, It's in the Eye of the Beholder." *China Daily*. November 8, 2014. https://www.chinadaily.com.cn/week-end/2014-11/08/content_18886853.htm.

Quigley, J. T. "World's Largest Building: Chengdu's New Century Global Center." *The Diplomat*. July 8, 2013. https://thediplomat.com/2013/07/worlds-larg-est-building-chengdus-new-century-global-center/.

Steinhardt, Nancy Shatzman. *Chinese Architecture: A History*. Princeton, NJ: Princeton University Press, 2019.

Wong, Edward. "Hotel Review: Commune by the Great Wall, Near Beijing." *New York Times*. November 4, 2009. https://www.nytimes.com/2009/11/08/travel/08check.html.

Wood, Graham. "This House in China Is Shaped Like a Giant Piano." *Business Insider*. June 25, 2012. https://www.businessinsider.com/chinas-pia-no-house-2012-6.

Index